GW00357412

July 23–August 22

Liberty Phi

LEO

OHEDITIONS

INTRODUCTION

A strology is all about the planets in our skies and what energy and characteristics influence us. From ancient times, people have wanted to understand the rhythms of life and looked to the skies and their celestial bodies for inspiration, and the ancient constellations are there in the 12 zodiac signs we recognise from astrology. The Ancient Greeks devised narratives related to myths and legends about their celestial ancestors, to which they referred to make decisions and choices. Roman mythology did the same and over the years these ancient wisdoms became refined into today's modern astrology.

The configuration of the planets in the sky at the time and place of our birth is unique to each and every one of us, and what this means and how it plays out throughout our lives is both fascinating and informative. Just knowing which planet rules your sun sign is the beginning of an exploratory journey that can provide you with a useful tool for life.

Understanding the meaning, energetic nature and power of each planet, where this sits in your birth chart and what this might mean is all important information and linked to your date, place and time of birth, relevant *only* to you. Completely individual, the way in which you can work with the power of the planets comes from understanding their qualities and how this might influence the position in which they sit in your chart.

What knowledge of astrology can give you is the tools for working out how a planetary pattern might influence you, because of its relationship to your particular planetary configuration and circumstances. Each sun sign has a set of characteristics linked to its ruling planet – for example, Leo is ruled by the Sun – and, in turn, to each of the 12 Houses (see page 81) that form the structure of every individual's birth chart (see page 78). Once you know the meanings of these and how these relate to different areas of your life, you can begin to work out what might be relevant to you when, for example, you read in a magazine horoscope that there's a Full Moon in Capricorn or that Jupiter is transiting Mars.

Each of the 12 astrological or zodiac sun signs is ruled by a planet (see page 52) and looking at a planet's characteristics will give you an indication of the influences brought to bear on each sign. It's useful to have a general understanding of these influences, because your birth chart includes many of them, in different house or planetary configurations, which gives you information about how uniquely *you* you are. Also included in this book are the minor planets (see page 102), also relevant to the information your chart provides.

LEO

Our sun sign is determined by the date of our birth wherever we are born, and if you are a Leo you were born between July 23rd and August 22nd. Bear in mind, however, that if you were born on one or other of those actual dates it's worth checking your *time* of birth, if you know it, against the year you were born and where. That's because no one is born 'on the cusp' (see page 78) and because there will be a moment on those days when Cancer shifts to Leo, and Leo shifts to Virgo. It's well worth a check, especially if you've never felt quite convinced that the characteristics of your designated sun sign match your own.

The constellation of Leo is one of the biggest in our skies and consists of 13 stars, the brightest of which is Alpha Leonis, or Regulus (the Latin for little king), which is also one of the brightest stars in our night sky. In Greek mythology, this was the indestructible lion of Nemea which Hercules was sent to kill, and he did by strangulation with his bare hands.

Leo is ruled by the Sun, not strictly a planet but a star, but definitely the ruler of the heavens and our galaxy. The Sun represents the life force on which we all depend, and in everyone's birth chart represents the masculine.

A fire sign (like Aries and Sagittarius), Leo is expansive in attitude, optimistic about life and extraverted in the expression of their ego. Leo is also a fixed sign (like Taurus, Scorpio and Aquarius) and once they've assumed a position on something, it can take them a while to reconsider or change it. This can make Leo come across as very emphatic in their beliefs and opinions, but they are also highly creative, which is a real boon when thinking something through again and problem-solving. Among the most loyal of friends, once they've made a commitment they stick to it, whether this is driving you to the airport at 4am for a flight or cooking a meal when you're sick. And they can be generous to a fault, wanting to share the bounty of their world, even if this means the last chocolate in the box.

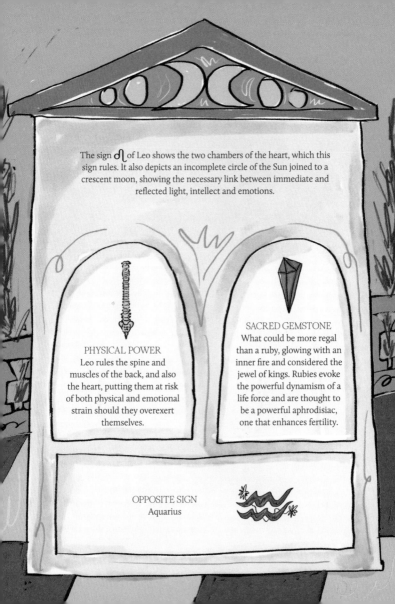

The sign ♌ of Leo shows the two chambers of the heart, which this sign rules. It also depicts an incomplete circle of the Sun joined to a crescent moon, showing the necessary link between immediate and reflected light, intellect and emotions.

PHYSICAL POWER
Leo rules the spine and muscles of the back, and also the heart, putting them at risk of both physical and emotional strain should they overexert themselves.

SACRED GEMSTONE
What could be more regal than a ruby, glowing with an inner fire and considered the jewel of kings. Rubies evoke the powerful dynamism of a life force and are thought to be a powerful aphrodisiac, one that enhances fertility.

OPPOSITE SIGN
Aquarius

L eo is depicted by the lion, the king of the jungle, and to be as brave as a lion is an important accolade for this sign, as they tend to see themselves as a lionheart, courageous in the face of adversity.

Those born under the sign of Leo are seldom easy to miss and you may well hear their roar before you see them because they are not the quietest of personalities. This roar may be metaphorical, but Leo seldom has any trouble standing up for themselves, or for others they care about. That big heart has a tendency to look out for the underdog, defending those who can't quite manage it for themselves, which is one of their most attractive features. Leos are usually loyal to a fault and the only downside of this is that they can sometimes be taken for a ride, especially if they are feted and complimented by others less authentic than themselves. As a fixed sign Leo isn't the most savvy or intuitive when it comes to the intentions of others, and can be susceptible to flattery and easily manipulated. They also have a tendency to see the best and ignore the worst in a situation, which can aggravate it. Leos do however learn by experience and over time, as they mature, this is less likely to happen.

Ruled by the Sun, Leos tend to see themselves as the centre of the universe. In some ways it's to be admired, this ability to place themselves at the centre of everything, but it's often necessary for Leo to learn that sometimes other people's needs and feelings should be prioritised, in order to coexist harmoniously in this world. They may need this pointed out, but fortunately Leo is by nature imaginative enough to learn to see things from another's point of view, and develop the empathy they need to take this on board. Leo isn't by nature possessive with their possessions or emotions, and often love to share what they see as their good fortune. This generosity of spirit and their optimistic nature can win over many of life's cynics or sceptics. That's the beauty of the Sun, it can warm others too and Leo will seldom give up, believing that no one or nothing is a lost cause.

What makes their me-first attitude so forgivable is that there's a lovely energy to Leo and they are usually good-natured, life-affirming people to be around. They're generous to a fault, attractive and stimulating company and often full of contagious optimism, making them hard to resist. A sought-out lover, friend or work companion, they bring sunshine into the lives of others. Not only do Leos have a big heart, they consequently tend to have big emotions and feel things intensely. And this can mask a hidden sensitivity that is sometimes overlooked because that roar can drown out what really needs to be said – and then the lion tends to retreat to lick his paws until recovered.

THE MOON IN YOUR CHART

While your zodiac sign is your sun sign, making you a sun sign Leo, the Moon also plays a role in your birth chart and if you know the time and place of your birth, along with your birth date, you can get your birth chart done (see page 78). From this you can discover in which zodiac sign your Moon is positioned in your chart.

The Moon reflects the characteristics of who you are at the time of your birth, your innate personality, how you express yourself and how you are seen by others. This is in contrast to our sun sign which indicates the more dominant characteristics we reveal as we travel through life. The Moon also represents the feminine in our natal chart (the Sun the masculine) and the sign in which our Moon falls can indicate how we express the feminine side of our personality. Looking at the two signs together in our charts immediately creates a balance.

MOON IN LEO

The Moon spends roughly 2.5 days in each zodiac sign as it moves through all 12 signs during its monthly cycle. This means that the Moon is regularly in Leo, and it can be useful to know when this occurs and in particular when we have a New Moon or a Full Moon in Leo because these are especially good times for you to focus your energy and intentions.

A New Moon is always the start of a new cycle, an opportunity to set new intentions for the coming month, and when this is in your own sign, Leo, you can benefit from this additional energy and support. The Full Moon is an opportunity to reflect on the culmination of your earlier intentions.

NEW MOON
IN LEO AFFIRMATION

'I will keep my courage safe in my heart even when
I fear it will fail me, trusting in this strength to guide
and support me on my journey.'

FULL MOON
IN LEO AFFIRMATION

'In the Full Moon's reflected light I will see more
clearly the success of my efforts, allowing myself to
learn from what hasn't turned out as I had hoped or
expected.'

LEO HEALTH

L eo rules the back and the spine, which can become weakened and subject to strain unless kept strong and supple. The heart is also ruled by Leo and this too can feel things deeply, emotionally and physically, and also needs to be kept strong. The heart may be a muscle, but it can also be affected by our emotions and Leo has to remember to maintain a balance in life, as working and playing hard can catch up with the lion.

Most Leos enjoy physical exercise in one form or another, but it's over competitive exercise because they love to win! Team sports can provide a good outlet for this as well as their social and leadership energies. They do however have a tendency to overdo things, even exercise, and can sometimes aggravate old aches and pains by trying to exercise them away. Taking advice from a physical trainer or doctor doesn't always sit easy with Leo either, as they feel sure that no one knows better than they what their body needs. Suggesting that they balance high-impact sports with something gentler to reduce stress might not meet with Leo's immediate approval, but one of the best things they can learn is to listen to experts and take note, particularly if advised about the health of their heart.

POWER UP
YOUR LEO
ENERGY

There are often moments or periods when we feel uninspired, demotivated and low in energy. At these times it's worth working with your innate sun sign energy to power up again, and paying attention to what Leo relishes and needs can help support both physical and mental health.

As a fire sign Leo can have a tendency to burn the candle at both ends (at work, at play or both) and seldom notices the encroaching signs of burnout until it's too late. Work-life balance isn't a Leo trait; their enthusiasm can take precedence over self-care and it may take something specific, like an injury, to make them notice the need to prioritise their health, at least for a while, in order to reinvigorate. Leo makes a poor patient, impatient and irritated about slowing down.

Better then for Leo to be a little more alert to those signs that it's time to re-energise with some time off and time out. Because Leo so often functions on high alert and enjoys the exhilaration of stress, elevated heart rate and even palpitations can begin to feel normal. Factoring in gentle daily exercise can help improve sleep at night, something that can elude hyped-up Leo. And tone down the high-octane socialisation, just for a while, in order to recalibrate the stress thermostat. As king of the jungle Leo often feels the need to be on full power, all the time, but even the lion needs his den in which to rest.

Regular nutritious meals will also help recharge the batteries as Leo often forgets to eat, or eats on the run, or late at night, skewing their digestive systems. A balanced combination of protein and carbohydrate, vitamins and minerals, will help to restore Leo energy. The recommendation for Leo is to avoid a fatty diet, as too much cholesterol won't help their heart, while a diet that includes onions and garlic will. When it comes to grains, don't overdo the gluten either, but make other choices for pasta, rice and bread, and find carbs in lentils, pulses, Brazil nuts and sunflower seeds, instead.

With herbs and spices, Leo's appetite is often stimulated by orange zest, rosemary, parsley and dill, while ginger and paprika will help restore a little fire and help power up the appetite to support Leo's physical and emotional health again.

Utilise a New Moon in Leo with a ritual to set your intentions and power up: light a candle, use essential oil of ylang ylang to stimulate your mood and concentration (this oil blends well with grounding cardamom and gentle rose), focus your thoughts on the change you wish to see and meditate on this. Place your gemstone (see page 13) in the moonlight. Write down your intentions and keep in a safe place. Meditate on the New Moon in Leo affirmation (see page 21).

At a Full Moon in Leo you will have the benefit of the Sun's reflected light to illuminate what is working for you and what you can let go, because the Full Moon brings clarity. Take the time to meditate on the Full Moon in Leo affirmation (see page 21). Light a candle, place your gemstone in the moonlight and make a note of your thoughts and feelings, strengthened by the Moon in your sign.

LEO'S SPIRITUAL HOME

K nowing where to go to replenish your soul and recharge
your batteries both physically and spiritually is important
and worth serious consideration. The lion can live almost
anywhere because they are social animals who find their own
savannah and pride of lions to share a life with wherever they go.
This is because socialisation is key to Leo's personality, although
they do like to be the leader of the pack.

Wherever they hail from, there are also a number of countries
where Leo will feel comfortable, whether they choose to go there to
live, work or just take a holiday. The countries of France, Colombia,
Japan and Vietnam are all attractive to Leo's fiery energy, and they
will easily find somewhere that resonates with this.

On holiday, while some Leos prefer to be active, for others this
is a chance to really chill out and relax, possibly in sunshine, whether
this is on an exotic beach or ski slope. There's always likely to be
an element of luxury though as Leo doesn't like to slum it, so even
if it's the hippie trail there'll be a high-end resort to compensate
somewhere.

L E O

WOMAN

Leo woman is a law unto herself, a queen (drama or otherwise) in her own kingdom, and she responds best to those who remember this. She thrives on admiration and there's much to admire about her gusto for life, and willingness to include others on the ride. It can sometimes be hard to keep up with her ideas and enthusiasm but, being a fixed sign, these can remain pretty constant, with her at their centre.

Easy to spot because she has a style all of her own, Leo women often choose strong colour blocks, or interesting accessories, to draw attention to themselves. Their attractive, striking appearance often sends a powerful message about who they are and their intentions. Of all the signs, Leo women are likely to power dress, and they love a designer label, even vintage, to show off their class. Not for them a pair of flats or flip flops, their preference is for killer heels, or kitten heels on a quiet day.

This is the woman you have on speed dial when you want to party or share fun times. Her instinct is to socialise, and quiet, intimate dinners are less likely than a rowdy karaoke night with the girls. When you need a leader for your pack, she's your girl. She's also generous to a fault, but don't take her for granted or exploit this, because while she'll give you her last cent should you need it, if you hurt her feelings or offend her in some way, she won't easily forgive this. As a fixed sign, once a line has been crossed, don't expect an easy path back, if at all, into her group.

Leo rules the 5th House of creativity (see page 83) and this is a woman who often directs her personal creativity to her offspring, should she choose to have children. Fiercely proud and often protective, she's likely to put a lot of energy into her progeny, seeing it as a way of investing in the future. When it comes to her own domestic life or leisure pastimes, that creativity is often seen in her home with beautiful objects or pieces of art crafted by herself.

One of the most loyal of the astrological sun signs, Leo women love the romance of love and love to be in love, and are seldom without a partner. They are romantic but, more than this, they like being one of a pair. Yes, they are happy to socialise but they also relish a one-to-one relationship on equal terms.

L E O

M A N

You may hear a Leo man across a crowded room before you see him. Holding court, telling the jokes, spinning the yarns and buying the drinks, he is social, generous and loves to be the centre of attention. Even shy Leos (yes, there are some) are quietly entertaining because they love an audience too.

Physically, Leo men often have a good mane of hair or facial hair that tends to be unruly rather than carefully trimmed. Similarly, the way they dress can be flamboyant, less the well-tailored suit and more about the patterned jumpers, comfortable trousers and unbuttoned shirts; they often look the creative types that they are. Leo gestures are often rather expansive and they move in a determined fashion, whether this is across a room or up a mountain. Their physical vigour is part of who they are, whether prowling or pursuing their objective. Most have a competitive streak, and will always be aware of the competition, often working out who is the top cat as they unconsciously scan the hierarchy in the room.

While given to the occasionally dramatic gesture, and Leo men are often prone to a hint of drama, he is also someone who invests heavily in life and his legacy. Leo rules the 5th House of creativity and this includes the creativity required for procreation. This is a man who takes great pride in his legacy, his offspring in particular, and has high hopes that they too will invest in the future and continue the family line. If there are no children, then this creativity is likely to be put towards pursuing something long lasting, in art or publishing, architecture or competitive performance in sport or the arts. Leo loves to leave his mark on the world in one way or another.

As a lover, friend or work colleague, Leo is usually a popular, big-hearted, loyal and fun companion, whose fixed attitude can make him a stickler for rules and conventions of society, but who is unlikely to ever let you down.

LEO IN LOVE

Ruled by the Sun, Leo likes to radiate love and falls in love readily and often. This is not a fickle sign, but a sign that just sees love as one of the many benefits of life and wants to enjoy it, one-to-one with a partner. This can make them inclined to finding 'the one' a priority. This is partly because of Leo's instinct for continuing their legacy, so a family and children is often on their long-term agenda, and if necessary they will play the field to find the best bet for this outcome. And as a precursor to love, Leo approaches dating as a fun activity, something to be enjoyed for its own sake. In this way they can explore the more enduring side of a prospective partner's personality because ultimately they are looking to the long term. They are also looking for someone to reward their attention with attention in return. Leo is unlikely to fall in love with anyone who isn't 100 per cent focused on them.

LEO AS
A LOVER

Open-hearted, trusting, affectionate and sensual, sex for a Leo is seldom half-hearted but a three-course meal to be savoured and enjoyed, and it doesn't take much to turn them on. That's not to say that Leos aren't discerning, they are, but as long as they are given authentic, loving attention, they are programmed to respond. Surprisingly, Leo sometimes harbours a degree of self-doubt so need full-on admiration needs to be expressed so that their confidence isn't hampered by insecurity. If that happens, it can take a while to coax the lion out of its den once more.

Leo isn't casual about love, even if they take their time. They like the setting and ambience to be right, and also have a taste for the more luxurious side of life. And because there's always an element of performance, even if there's only an audience of one, this audience needs to be appreciative of Leo's efforts (did I mention the occasional insecurity?). One of the less sexually adventurous sun signs, Leo can sometimes be encouraged to let their eroticism shine a little more once they are secure.

If this all sounds a bit of a contradiction, remember that Leo's big personality is mostly a performance to ensure they remain king or queen of the jungle. Underneath they are as human as anyone, with a deep need to be loved. It's often only then that the lion reaches their full potential as a lover, but it's well worth the gentle encouragement. Once committed, Leo is one of the most loyal of lovers, and will continue to want to please and satisfy their partner, particularly to prevent any inclination to stray. Leo's commitment to their legacy is part of this; they usually want to create an enduring family unit.

WHAT'S IN LEO'S BEDSIDE CABINET?

For sensuous massage, oil scented with bergamot and grapefruit

A state-of-the-art vibrator to make a lover purr or roar

A well-thumbed copy of the *Kama Sutra*

WHICH SIGN
SUITS LEO?

I n relationships with a Leo, the sun sign of the other person and
the ruling planet of that sign can bring out the best, or sometimes
the worst, in a lover. Knowing what might spark, smoulder or
suffocate love is worth closer investigation, but always remember
that sun sign astrology is only a starting point for any relationship.

LEO AND ARIES

Two fire signs, they understand each other's warmth and energy and it can be a powerful partnership as long as Mars understands that the Sun always needs to shine and to be appreciated for doing so.

LEO AND TAURUS

The Sun and Venus create a lovely harmonious partnership, just as long as Leo doesn't try to dominate Taurus' more gentle, earthy nature but instead fires it up so that they are emotionally stronger together than apart.

LEO AND GEMINI

While Leo loves Gemini's quick mind and their airiness can oxygenate their fire, it can also blow it out, and that Mercurial influence can sometimes prove too fickle and inattentive, which makes them feel insecure.

LEO AND CANCER

Cancer's nurturing Moon is often more than happy to reflect Leo's sunlight and the crab's tenacity makes the lion feel secure, just as long as they don't overwhelm each other with their respective needs.

LEO AND LEO

Although this pairing can sometimes just be too much for both, they do recognise and appreciate exactly what the other wants. But then it becomes a question of balance and to learn the give and take when necessary.

LEO AND VIRGO

Virgo's earthiness loves to be warmed by the Sun, so this can be a happy pairing as long as Leo accepts that Virgo may not always respond immediately to their enthusiasms and will sometimes question their more flamboyant ideas.

LEO AND LIBRA

Libra can bring balance to this relationship. Their Venus is readily attracted to Leo's Sun and they both have a love of luxury, but it can run into trouble unless they accept that boundaries might be necessary around the family budget.

LEO AND SCORPIO

Watery Scorpio can put a dampener on the Sun's fire, so this isn't generally considered an ideal partnership except for the fact that Leo is all about creativity and Scorpio is about regeneration, so they have this understanding at an unconscious level.

LEO AND SAGITTARIUS

Sagittarius may just prove too boisterous and adventurous to make a long-lasting partnership with Leo's love of security possible, but they are both fire signs and full of enthusiasm so will always be friends if not lovers.

LEO AND CAPRICORN

Leo has a deep appreciation for Capricorn's sure-footed approach, but their ruling Saturn may just be too demanding of Leo, requiring them to proceed with more caution through life – although, in some instances, this creates the security they need.

LEO AND AQUARIUS

Airy, humanitarian Aquarius may not be able to meet the Sun's need for admiration and attention, although that slight unpredictability provided by their ruling planet Uranus will keep Leo on their toes.

LEO AND PISCES

Dreamy imaginative Pisces often inspires Leo's ideas, and the fishes can benefit from the Sun's fire to help bring them to fruition, so this can be a very creative partnership on all levels.

LEO AT
WORK

Leo loves to work, putting all their energy and enthusiasm into a project or towards a goal, and they can make excellent employees once they find an outlet for their talents. However, boredom and lack of stimulation can make them ineffectual, so many Leos tend to have a variety of careers in their lifetime. Making creative use of their experience and expertise, Leo tends to be successful at work and one of their drivers is remuneration because they do enjoy a bit of luxury in their lives.

Leo rules the 5th House of creativity (see page 83), making them capable of imagining something wonderful and taking it to fruition. Leo also has the drive to realise the most exciting of projects and this can make them a welcome participant in any team. The only downside is that some may not be prepared to compromise on their vision, so it can sometimes take careful negotiation on issues like budget or materials.

Often it's about the hustle and the hype, which can make Leo excellent at marketing and sales, as long as they are marketing and selling something they genuinely believe in, because this sign also has a broad streak of integrity and authenticity and they take great pride in this. In fact, one thing they are usually excellent at marketing and selling is themselves, so they tend to perform very well at interviews. Generally, Leo doesn't like to fail at anything and this helps motivate them to prepare carefully, even if diligence in this area seems an unlikely Leo trait.

As a team member, Leo helps to inspire and motivate others, always keen to encourage those less enthusiastic than themselves. This can make Leo excellent leaders too, as long as they are diligent about delegating and don't try and take all the credit for themselves. Leo often gravitates towards those careers which require a degree of performance, and giving a speech or a presentation holds little fear for most. In fact, theatrical careers like acting are often very appealing to a sign that positively looks for an audience. Also, teaching or the law, where there may be a captive audience to play to, can appeal. Anything with a public-facing role can work well for Leo, as they genuinely like to socialise with the rest of the jungle.

LEO AT HOME

It's often said that a Leo's home is their castle, and they are a sign that generally takes great pride in where they live, often using it to represent and showcase their worldly success, particularly in later life. Their creativity comes into its own here too and there may be an interesting mix of antique heirlooms, artfully combined with the modern or their own paintings or sculptures. Their decor is likely to be bold and bright too, with lots of windows allowing sunshine to illuminate their domestic world.

Leo's home is also likely to be comfortable and accommodating as they love to socialise, often with more than a nod to luxury in their choice of furniture, fixtures and fittings: beautiful drapes, deep-pile carpets, feather cushions, even if they are second hand or vintage. Leo will make smart, aesthetically pleasing choices to create a home that reflects their interests and taste. And it's also here that they like to entertain, whether this is for a kitchen supper, an intimate dinner or an anniversary party, because it's at home they can play best to their audience, as an hospitable and welcoming host, bringing lovers, friends, family and work colleagues into their personal space with charisma and charm.

It's also where Leo will raise their family, and they are likely to create one in one form or another even if they choose not to marry or have children, because families come in many forms. In fact, Leo often stays in the family home long after their ancestors or children have moved on, because nothing says legacy like a family home.

When it comes to sharing a Leo's home, they can be a tad possessive about their space and may need to reassert their king of the jungle status from time to time, but they can also be the most generous of housemates, keen to ensure that everyone benefits from their largesse.

FREE THE
SPIRIT

Understanding your own sun sign astrology is only part of the picture. It provides you with a template to examine and reflect on your own life's journey but also the context for this through your relationships with others, intimate or otherwise, and within the culture and environment in which you live.

Throughout time, the Sun and planets of our universe have kept to their paths and astrologers have used this ancient wisdom to understand the pattern of the universe. In this way, astrology is a tool to utilise these wisdoms, a way of helping make sense of the energies we experience as the planets shift in our skies.

'A physician without a knowledge of astrology has no right to call himself a physician,' said Hippocrates, the Greek physician born in 460 BC, who understood better than anyone how these psychic energies worked. As did Carl Jung, the 20th-century philosopher and psychoanalyst, because he said, 'Astrology represents the summation of all the psychological knowledge of antiquity.'

THE 10
PLANETS

SUN

RULES THE ASTROLOGICAL SIGN OF LEO

Although the Sun is officially a star, for the purpose
of astrology it's considered a planet. It is also the
centre of our universe and gives us both light and
energy; our lives are dependent on it and it embodies
our creative life force. As a life giver, the Sun is
considered a masculine entity, the patriarch and
ruler of the skies. Our sun sign is where we start our
astrological journey whichever sign it falls in, and as
long as we know which day of which month we were
born, we have this primary knowledge.

MOON

RULES THE ASTROLOGICAL SIGN OF CANCER

We now know that the Moon is actually a natural satellite of the Earth (the third planet from the Sun) rather than a planet but is considered such for the purposes of astrology. It's dependent on the Sun for its reflected light, and it is only through their celestial relationship that we can see it. In this way, the Moon in each of our birth charts depicts the feminine energy to balance the masculine Sun's life force, the ying to its yang. It is not an impotent or subservient presence, particularly when you consider how it gives the world's oceans their tides, the relentless energy of the ebb and flow powering up the seas. The Moon's energy also helps illuminate our unconscious desires, helping to bring these to the service of our self-knowledge.

MERCURY

RULES THE ASTROLOGICAL SIGNS OF GEMINI AND VIRGO

Mercury, messenger of the gods, has always been
associated with speed and agility, whether in body
or mind. Because of this, Mercury is considered to
be the planet of quick wit and anything requiring
verbal dexterity and the application of intelligence.
Those with Mercury prominent in their chart love
exchanging and debating ideas and telling stories
(often with a tendency to embellish the truth of a
situation), making them prominent in professions
where these qualities are valuable.

Astronomically, Mercury is the closest planet to the
Sun and moves around a lot in our skies. What's also
relevant is that several times a year Mercury appears
to be retrograde (see page 99) which has the effect of
slowing down or disrupting its influence.

VENUS

RULES THE ASTROLOGICAL SIGNS OF TAURUS AND LIBRA

The goddess of beauty, love and pleasure. Venus is
the second planet from the Sun and benefits from
this proximity, having received its positive vibes.
Depending on which astrological sign Venus falls in
your chart will influence how you relate to art and
culture and the opposite sex. The characteristics of
this sign will tell you all you need to know about
what you aspire to, where you seek and how you
experience pleasure, along with the types of lover you
attract. Again, partly depending on where it's placed,
Venus can sometimes increase self-indulgence which
can be a less positive aspect of a hedonistic life.

MARS

This big, powerful planet is fourth from the Sun and exerts an energetic force, powering up the characteristics of the astrological sign in which it falls in your chart. This will tell you how you assert yourself, whether your anger flares or smoulders, what might stir your passion and how you express your sexual desires. Mars will show you what works best for you to turn ideas into action, the sort of energy you might need to see something through and how your independent spirit can be most effectively engaged.

JUPITER

Big, bountiful Jupiter is the largest planet in our solar
system and fifth from the Sun. It heralds optimism,
generosity and general benevolence. Whichever sign
Jupiter falls in in your chart is where you will find
the characteristics for your particular experience of
luck, happiness and good fortune. Jupiter will show
you which areas to focus on to gain the most and
best from your life. Wherever Jupiter appears in your
chart it will bring a positive influence and when it's
prominent in our skies we all benefit.

SATURN

Saturn is considered akin to Old Father Time, with all the patience, realism and wisdom that archetype evokes. Sometimes called the taskmaster of the skies, its influence is all about how we handle responsibility and it requires that we graft and apply ourselves in order to learn life's lessons. The sixth planet from the Sun, Saturn's 'return' (see page 100) to its place in an individual's birth chart occurs approximately every 28 years. How self-disciplined you are about overcoming opposition or adversity will be influenced by the characteristics of the sign in which this powerful planet falls in your chart.

URANUS

The seventh planet from the Sun, Uranus is the planet of unpredictability, change and surprise, and whether you love or loathe the impact of Uranus will depend in part on which astrological sign it influences in your chart. How you respond to its influence is entirely up to the characteristics of the sign it occupies in your chart. Whether you see the change it heralds as a gift or a curse is up to you, but because it takes seven years to travel through a sign, its presence in a sign can influence a generation.

NEPTUNE

Neptune ruled the sea, and this planet is all about deep waters of mystery, imagination and secrets. It's also representative of our spiritual side so the characteristics of whichever astrological sign it occupies in your chart will influence how this plays out in your life. Neptune is the eighth planet from the Sun and its influence can be subtle and mysterious. The astrological sign in which it falls in your chart will indicate how you realise your vision, dream and goals. The only precaution is if it falls in an equally watery sign, creating a potential difficulty in distinguishing between fantasy and reality.

PLUTO

Pluto is the furthest planet from the Sun and exerts a regenerative energy that transforms but often requires destruction to erase what's come before in order to begin again. Its energy often lies dormant and then erupts, so the astrological sign in which it falls will have a bearing on how this might play out in your chart. Transformation can be very positive but also very painful. When Pluto's influence is strong, change occurs and how you react or respond to this will be very individual. Don't fear it, but reflect on how to use its energy to your benefit.

YOUR SUN SIGN

Your sun or zodiac sign is the one in which you were born, determined by the date of your birth. Your sun sign is ruled by a specific planet. For example, Leo is ruled by the Sun but Capricorn by Saturn, so we already have the first piece of information and the first piece of our individual jigsaw puzzle.

The next piece of the jigsaw is understanding that the energy of a particular planet in your birth chart (see page 78) plays out via the characteristics of the astrological sign in which it's positioned, and this is hugely valuable in understanding some of the patterns of your life. You may have your Sun in Leo, and a good insight into the characteristics of this sign, but what if you have Neptune in Cancer? Or Venus in Aries? Uranus in Virgo? Understanding the impact of these influences can help you reflect on the way you react or respond and the choices you can make, helping to ensure more positive outcomes.

If, for example, with Uranus in Taurus you are resistant to change, remind yourself that change is inevitable and can be positive, allowing you to work with it rather than against its influence. If you have Neptune in Virgo, it will bring a more spiritual element to this practical earth sign, while Mercury in Aquarius will enhance the predictive element of your analysis and judgement. The scope and range and useful aspect of having this knowledge is just the beginning of how you can utilise astrology to live your best life.

PLANETS IN TRANSIT

In addition, the planets do not stay still. They are said to transit (move) through the course of an astrological year. Those closest to us, like Mercury, transit quite regularly (every 88 days), while those further away, like Pluto, take much longer, in this case 248 years to come full circle. So the effects of each planet can vary depending on their position and this is why we hear astrologers talk about someone's Saturn return (see page 100), Mercury retrograde (see page 99) or about Capricorn (or other sun sign) 'weather'. This is indicative of an influence that can be anticipated and worked with and is both universal and personal. The shifting positions of the planets bring an influence to bear on each of us, linked to the position of our own planetary influences and how these have a bearing on each other. If you understand the nature of these planetary influences you can begin to work with, rather than against, them and this information can be very much to your benefit.

First, though, you need to take a look at the component parts of astrology, the pieces of your personal jigsaw, then you'll have the information you need to make sense of how your sun sign might be affected during the changing patterns of the planets.

YOUR BIRTH CHART

With the date, time and place of birth, you can easily find out where your (or anyone else's) planets are positioned from an online astrological chart programme (see page 110). This will give you an exact sun sign position, which you probably already know, but it can also be useful if you think you were born 'on the cusp' because it will give you an *exact* indication of what sign you were born in. In addition, this natal chart will tell you your Ascendant sign, which sign your Moon is in, along with the other planets specific to your personal and completely individual chart and the Houses (see page 81) in which the astrological signs are positioned.

A birth chart is divided into 12 sections, representing each of the 12 Houses (see pages 82–85) with your Ascendant or Rising sign always positioned in the 1st House, and the other 11 Houses running counter-clockwise from one to 12.

ASCENDANT OR RISING SIGN

Your Ascendant is a first, important part of the complexity of an individual birth chart. While your sun sign gives you an indication of the personality you will inhabit through the course of your life, it is your Ascendant or Rising sign – which is the sign rising at the break of dawn on the Eastern horizon at the time and on the date of your birth – that often gives a truer indication of how you will project your personality and consequently how the world sees you. So even though you were born a sun sign Leo, whatever sign your Ascendant is in, for example Cancer, will be read through the characteristics of this astrological sign.

Your Ascendant is always in your 1st House, which is the House of the Self (see page 82) and the other houses always follow the same consecutive astrological order. So if, for example, your Ascendant is Leo, then your second house is in Virgo, your third house in Libra, and so on. Each house has its own characteristics but how these will play out in your individual chart will be influenced by the sign positioned in it.

Opposite your Ascendant is your Descendant sign, positioned in the 7th House (see page 84) and this shows what you look for in a partnership, your complementary 'other half' as it were. There's always something intriguing about what the Descendant can help us to understand, and it's worth knowing yours and being on the lookout for it when considering a long-term marital or business partnership.

THE
12
HOUSES

While each of the 12 Houses represent different aspects of our lives, they are also ruled by one of the 12 astrological signs, giving each house its specific characteristics. When we discover, for example, that we have Capricorn in the 12th House, this might suggest a pragmatic or practical approach to spirituality. Or, if you had Gemini in your 6th House, this might suggest a rather airy approach to organisation.

1ST HOUSE

RULED BY ARIES

The first impression you give walking into
a room, how you like to be seen, your sense
of self and the energy with which you
approach life.

2ND HOUSE

RULED BY TAURUS

What you value, including what you own
that provides your material security; your
self-value and work ethic, how you earn
your income.

3RD HOUSE

RULED BY GEMINI

How you communicate through words,
deeds and gestures; also how you learn and
function in a group, including within your
own family.

4 TH HOUSE

RULED BY CANCER

This is about your home, your security
and how you take care of yourself and
your family; and also about those family
traditions you hold dear.

5 TH HOUSE

RULED BY LEO

Creativity in all its forms, including fun
and eroticism, intimate relationships and
procreation, self-expression
and positive fulfilment.

6 TH HOUSE

RULED BY VIRGO

How you organise your daily routine, your
health, your business affairs, and how you
are of service to others, from those
in your family to the workplace.

7 TH HOUSE

RULED BY LIBRA

This is about partnerships and shared
goals, whether marital or in business,
and what we look for in these to
complement ourselves.

8 TH HOUSE

RULED BY SCORPIO

Regeneration, through death and rebirth,
and also our legacy and how this might be
realised through sex, procreation
and progeny.

9 TH HOUSE

RULED BY SAGITTARIUS

Our world view, cultures outside our
own and the bigger picture beyond our
immediate horizon, to which we travel
either in body or mind.

♌

10TH HOUSE

RULED BY CAPRICORN

Our aims and ambitions in life, what we aspire
to and what we're prepared to do to achieve it;
this is how we approach our working lives.

11TH HOUSE

RULED BY AQUARIUS

The house of humanity and our
friendships, our relationships with the
wider world, our tribe or group to which
we feel an affiliation.

12TH HOUSE

RULED BY PISCES

Our spiritual side resides here. Whether this
is religious or not, it embodies our inner life,
beliefs and the deeper connections we forge.

THE FOUR
ELEMENTS

The 12 astrological signs are divided into four groups,
representing the four elements: fire, water, earth and air.
This gives each of the three signs in each group additional
characteristics.

FIRE

ARIES ❧ LEO ❧ SAGITTARIUS

Embodying warmth, spontaneity and enthusiasm.

♌ LEO

WATER

CANCER ❧ SCORPIO ❧ PISCES

Embodying a more feeling, spiritual and intuitive side.

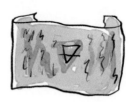

EARTH

TAURUS ⚹ VIRGO ⚹ CAPRICORN

Grounded and sure-footed and sometimes rather stubborn.

AIR

GEMINI ✿ LIBRA ✿ AQUARIUS

Flourishing in the world of vision, ideas and perception.

FIXED, CARDINAL OR MUTABLE?

The 12 signs are further divided into three groups of four, giving additional characteristics of being fixed, cardinal or mutable. These represent the way in which they respond to situations.

FIXED

TAURUS, LEO, SCORPIO AND AQUARIUS ARE FIXED SIGNS

Their energy tends to be steady and they are less reactive, more responsive, although they can have a tendency to be resistant to change and need encouragement.

CARDINAL

ARIES, CANCER, LIBRA AND CAPRICORN ARE CARDINAL SIGNS

Their energy is often instinctive and action-oriented, enabling them to get things started, although there's sometimes a tendency to fail to carry things through.

MUTABLE

GEMINI, VIRGO, SAGITTARIUS AND PISCES ARE MUTABLE SIGNS

The clue here is their adaptability and responsiveness to change, which they don't fear, and readiness to listen to and embrace new ideas.

MERCURY RETROGRADE

This occurs several times over the astrological year and lasts for around four weeks, with a shadow week either side (a quick Google search will tell you the forthcoming dates). It's important what sign Mercury is in while it's retrograde, because its impact will be affected by the characteristics of that sign. For example, if Mercury is retrograde in Gemini, the sign of communication that is ruled by Mercury, the effect will be keenly felt in all areas of communication. However, if Mercury is retrograde in Aquarius, which rules the house of friendships and relationships, this may keenly affect our communication with large groups, or if in Sagittarius, which rules the house of travel, it could affect travel itineraries and encourage us to check our documents carefully.

Mercury retrograde can also be seen as an opportunity to pause, review or reconsider ideas and plans, to regroup, recalibrate and recuperate, and generally to take stock of where we are and how we might proceed. In our fast-paced 24/7 lives, Mercury retrograde can often be a useful opportunity to slow down and allow ourselves space to restore some necessary equilibrium.

SATURN RETURN

When the planet Saturn returns to the place in your chart that it occupied at the time of your birth, it has an impact. This occurs roughly every 28 years, so we can see immediately that it correlates with ages that we consider representative of different life stages and when we might anticipate change or adjustment to a different era. At 28 we can be considered at full adult maturity, probably established in our careers and relationships, maybe with children; at 56 we have reached middle age and are possibly at another of life's crossroads; and at 84, we might be considered at the full height of our wisdom, our lives almost complete. If you know the time and place of your birth date, an online Saturn return calculator can give you the exact timing.

It will also be useful to identify in which astrological sign Saturn falls in your chart, which will help you reflect on its influence, as both influences can be very illuminating about how you will experience and manage the impact of its return. Often the time leading up to a personal Saturn return is a demanding one, but the lessons learnt help inform the decisions made about how to progress your own goals. Don't fear this period, but work with its influence: knowledge is power and Saturn has a powerful energy you can harness should you choose.

THE MINOR
PLANETS

Sun sign astrology seldom makes mention of these 'minor' planets that also orbit the Sun, but increasingly their subtle influence is being referenced. If you have had your birth chart done (if you know your birth time and place you can do this online) you will have access to this additional information.

Like the 10 main planets on the previous pages, these 18 minor entities will also be positioned in an astrological sign, bringing their energy to bear on these characteristics. You may, for example, have Fortuna in Leo, or Diana in Sagittarius. Look to these for their subtle influences on your birth chart and life via the sign they inhabit, all of which will serve to animate and resonate further the information you can reference on your own personal journey.

AESCULAPIA

Jupiter's grandson and a powerful healer, Aesculapia was taught by Chiron and influences us in what could be life-saving action, realised through the characteristics of the sign in which it falls in our chart.

BACCHUS

Jupiter's son Bacchus is similarly benevolent but can sometimes lack restraint in the pursuit of pleasure. How this plays out in your chart is dependent on the sign in which it falls.

APOLLO

Jupiter's son, gifted in art, music and healing, Apollo rides the Sun across the skies. His energy literally lights up the way in which you inspire others, characterised by the sign in which it falls in your chart.

CERES

Goddess of agriculture and mother of Proserpina, Ceres is associated with the seasons and how we manage cycles of change in our lives. This energy is influenced by the sign in which it falls in our chart.

CHIRON

Teacher of the gods, Chiron knew all about healing herbs and medical practices and he lends his energy to how we tackle the impossible or the unthinkable, that which seems difficult to do.

DIANA

Jupiter's independent daughter was allowed to run free without the shackles of marriage. Where this falls in your birth chart will indicate what you are not prepared to sacrifice in order to conform.

CUPID

Son of Venus. The sign into which Cupid falls will influence how you inspire love and desire in others, not always appropriately and sometimes illogically but it can still be an enduring passion.

FORTUNA

Jupiter's daughter, who is always shown blindfolded, influences your fated role in other people's lives, how you show up for them without really understanding why, and at the right time.

HYGEIA

Daughter of Aesculapia and also associated with health, Hygeia is about how you anticipate risk and the avoidance of unwanted outcomes. The way you do this is characterised by the sign in which Hygeia falls.

MINERVA

Another of Jupiter's daughters, depicted by an owl, will show you via the energy given to a particular astrological sign in your chart how you show up at your most intelligent and smart. How you operate intellectually.

JUNO

Juno was the wife of Jupiter and her position in your chart will indicate where you will make a commitment in order to feel safe and secure. It's where you might seek protection in order to flourish.

OPS

The wife of Saturn, Ops saved the life of her son Jupiter by giving her husband a stone to eat instead of him. Her energy in our chart enables us to find positive solutions to life's demands and dilemmas.

PANACEA

Gifted with healing powers, Panacea
provides us with a remedy for all ills
and difficulties, and how this plays
out in your life will depend on the
characteristics of the astrological sign
in which her energy falls.

PSYCHE

Psyche, Venus' daughter-in-law, shows
us that part of ourselves that is easy to
love and endures through adversity,
and your soul that survives death and
flies free, like the butterfly that
depicts her.

PROSERPINA

Daughter of Ceres, abducted by Pluto,
Proserpina has to spend her life divided
between earth and the underworld and
she represents how we bridge the gulf
between different and difficult aspects
of our lives.

SALACIA

Neptune's wife, Salacia stands on
the seashore bridging land and sea,
happily bridging the two realities.
In your chart, she shows how you
can harmoniously bring two sides of
yourself together.

VESTA

Daughter of Saturn, Vesta's job was to protect Rome and in turn she was protected by vestal virgins. Her energy influences how we manage our relationships with competitive females and male authority figures.

VULCAN

Vulcan was a blacksmith who knew how to control fire and fashion metal into shape, and through the sign in which it falls in your chart will show you how you control your passion and make it work for you.

FURTHER READING

Jung's Studies in Astrology: Prophecies, Magic and the Qualities of Time,

Liz Greene, Routledge (2018)

Lunar Oracle: Harness the Power of the Moon,

Liberty Phi, OH Editions (2021)

Metaphysics of Astrology: Why Astrology Works,

Ivan Antic, Independently published (2020)

Parkers' Astrology: The Definitive Guide to Using Astrology in Every Aspect of Your Life,

Julia and Derek Parker, Dorling Kindersley (2020)

USEFUL WEBSITES

Alicebellastrology.com
Astro.com
Astrology.com
Cafeastrology.com
Costarastrology.com
Jessicaadams.com

USEFUL APPS

Astro Future
Co-Star
Moon
Sanctuary
Time Nomad
Time Passages

ACKNOWLEDGEMENTS

Thanks are due to my Taurean publisher Kate Pollard for commissioning this Astrology Oracle series, to Piscean Matt Tomlinson for his careful editing, and to Evi O Studio for their beautiful design and illustrations.

ABOUT THE AUTHOR

As a sun sign Aquarius Liberty Phi loves to explore the world and has lived on three different continents, currently residing in North America. Their Gemini moon inspires them to communicate their love of astrology and other esoteric practices while Leo rising helps energise them. Their first publication, also released by OH Editions, is a box set of 36 oracle cards and accompanying guide, entitled *Lunar Oracle: Harness the Power of the Moon*.

Published in 2023 by OH Editions,
an imprint of Welbeck Non-Fiction Ltd,
part of the Welbeck Publishing Group.
Offices in London, 20 Mortimer Street, London, W1T 3JW,
and Sydney, 205 Commonwealth Street, Surry Hills, 2010.
www.welbeckpublishing.com

Design © 2023 OH Editions
Text © 2023 Liberty Phi
Illustrations © 2023 Evi O. Studio

A CIP catalogue record for this book is available from the British Library.

ISBN 978-1-91431-797-2

Publisher: Kate Pollard
Editor: Sophie Elletson
In-house editor: Matt Tomlinson
Designer: Evi O. Studio
Illustrator: Evi O. Studio
Production controller: Jess Brisley
Printed and bound by Leo Paper

MIX
Paper | Supporting
responsible forestry
FSC® C020056
www.fsc.org

10 9 8 7 6 5 4 3 2 1